Laura Bush

By Wil Mara

Consultant
Jeanne Clidas, Ph.D.
National Reading Consultant
and
Professor of Reading, SUNY Brockport

Children's Press ®
A Division of Scholastic Inc.
New York   Toronto   London   Auckland   Sydney
Mexico City   New Delhi   Hong Kong
Danbury, Connecticut

Designer: Herman Adler Design
Photo Researcher: Caroline Anderson
The photo on the cover shows Laura Bush.

Library of Congress Cataloging-in-Publication Data

Mara, Wil.
  Laura Bush / by Wil Mara.
     p. cm. — (Rookie biographies)
Includes index.
Summary: An introduction to the life of the former Texas librarian and teacher
who, as the wife of the forty-third president, became first lady in 2001.
  ISBN 0-516-22854-4 (lib. bdg.)   0-516-27839-8 (pbk.)
  1. Bush, Laura Welch, 1946—Juvenile literature. 2. Presidents'
spouses—United States—Biography—Juvenile literature. [1. Bush, Laura
Welch, 1946- 2. First ladies. 3. Women—Biography.] I. Title. II.
Series: Rookie biography
  E904.B87 M37 2003
  973.931'092—dc21

2002015162

CHILDREN'S PRESS, AND ROOKIE BIOGRAPHIES™, and associated
logos are trademarks and or registered trademarks of Grolier Publishing
Co., Inc. SCHOLASTIC and associated logos are trademarks and or
registered trademarks of Scholastic Inc.
1 2 3 4 5 6 7 8 9 10 R 12 11 10 09 08 07 06 05 04 03

Do you like to learn new things?

Laura Bush has spent much of her life showing children how much fun learning can be.

She was born in Midland, Texas, on November 4, 1946. She was the only child of Harold and Jenna Welch.

8

Laura spent a lot of time reading when she was a child. She did not have any brothers or sisters to play with. She taught herself many things.

Laura began teaching in elementary schools in Texas in the 1960s. She also became a librarian (lye-BRARE-ee-uhn). A librarian is someone who helps you to find books in a library.

12

In 1977, she met a man named George. Laura and George married a few months later. They had twin daughters. Their names are Jenna and Barbara.

George was part of a famous family. His father was a politician (pol-uh-TISH-uhn). A politician is someone who helps to run a town, state, or country.

15

George also wanted to be
a politician. Eventually, he
became the governor of the
state of Texas.

Now Laura Bush was famous, too! She was the governor's wife. People called her the "First Lady of Texas."

19

Laura Bush used her fame to help children. She spoke on television. She also spoke in schools and libraries. She was able to tell a lot of people how important it is to read and to learn.

She also helped create the
Texas Book Festival. Libraries
in Texas have received over one
million dollars because of it.

Laura's husband became the
43rd president of the United
States in the year 2000.

She went from being the First
Lady of Texas to the First Lady
of the United States!

Laura Bush still talks to moms and dads. She wants to make sure their children are ready for school when they are old enough to go.

Thousands of children will do better in school because of Laura Bush.

Words You Know

Laura Bush

librarian

politician

30

governor

president

Texas

Texas Book Festival

Index

About the Author

More than fifty published books bear Wil Mara's name. He has written both fiction and nonfiction, for both children and adults. He lives with his family in northern New Jersey.

Photo Credits

Photographs © 2003: AP/Wide World Photos: 4 (Peter Cosgrove), 23, 31 bottom right (Ron Edmonds), 29, 30 top (Bill Haber), 25, 31 top right (Doug Mills); Classmates.Com Yearbook Archives: 8; Corbis Images/Richard Hutchings: 3; Getty Images: cover (Michael Evans), 24 (Win McNamee/Reuters), 12, 31 top left (Newsmakers), 20 (Michael Williams/Newsmakers); The Image Works: 11, 15, 16, 30 bottom left, 30 bottom right (Bob Daemmrich), 26 (Richard Lord), 19 (Tannen Maury); Tom Stack & Associates, Inc./Byron Augustin: 7, 31 bottom left.